LOOPS & TWISTS

LEISURE ARTS, INC. Maumelle, Arkansas

Introduction

Loop yarn is a unique and different type of yarn. It comes with stitches already made and is the perfect craft yarn to finger knit for kids and adults. This yarn removes the necessity to use knitting needles or crochet hooks, and even those who don't know how to knit can easily learn how to knit with this yarn. No more excuses such as "I can't knit or crochet", because with this yarn, anybody can and will be able to knit. It's the ultimate finger knitting yarn!

In this book, we will start with the basic stitches and terms and apply them one by one. We will use different techniques through this book, resulting in a collection of items anyone can make. The patterns in the book range from a scarf to a pet bed, and we'll work through them each step of the way.....and if you still need assistance, there are videos to guide you through, too! Kristi Simpson demonstrates each stitch used in this book, helpful tips for each item and many helpful tips and tricks on her website: www.KristiSimpson.net. Feel free to use those videos to learn, teach and complete each project in this book.

Now, grab that fluffy, soft, loopy yarn and let's get started!

Contents

COMMON TERMINOLOGY/DEFINITIONS

Cast on — the amount of loops used to begin a project

Working yarn — the yarn that is coming from the ball (consists of loops)

Stitch — the active loops forming the project

Knit (K) — with the working yarn in the **back**, pass the next loop on the working yarn from **back** to **front** through the next stitch

Purl (P) — with the working yarn in the **front**, pass the working yarn from **front** to **back** through the next stitch

Bind off — securing the stitch(es) so the piece doesn't unravel; it can be used within a pattern and will be used on the last row to finish

Cable — crossing loops as specified to create a twisted look in the work

Working in the round — each round is made in a circular motion instead of back and forth in rows

Knit 2 Together (K2 tog) — making one stitch from 2 stitches by overlapping them and knitting them together

★ — work instructions following ★ as many **more** times as indicated in addition to the first time

BASIC	Projects using basic stitches. May include basic increases and decreases.
EASY	Projects may include simple stitch patterns, color work, and/or shaping.
INTERMEDIATE	Projects may include involved stitch patterns, color work, and/or shaping.
COMPLEX	Projects may include complex stitch patterns, color work, and/or shaping using a variety of techniques and stitches simultaneously.

Yarn Weight Symbol & Names	SUPER FINE 1	FINE 2	LIGHT 3	MEDIUM 4	BULKY 5	SUPER BULKY 6	JUMBO 7
Type of Yarns in Category	Sock, Fingering, Baby	Sport, Baby	DK, Light Worsted	Worsted, Afghan, Aran	Chunky, Craft, Rug	Bulky, Roving	Jumbo, Roving

Scarf

BASIC

In this pattern, you will learn several techniques, tips and tricks on how to get started with this unique yarn. We are going to begin with a pretty and simple scarf so you can practice and perfect the basics before we move on.

Approximate Finished Size:

7½" x 60½" (19 cm x 153.5 cm)

SHOPPING LIST

Yarn (Jumbo Weight)

JUMBO 7

[6.4 ounces, 18 yards (180 grams, 16 meters) per skein]:

- ☐ 1 skein

Additional Supplies

- ☐ Scissors
- ☐ Large eye tapestry or yarn needle

INSTRUCTIONS

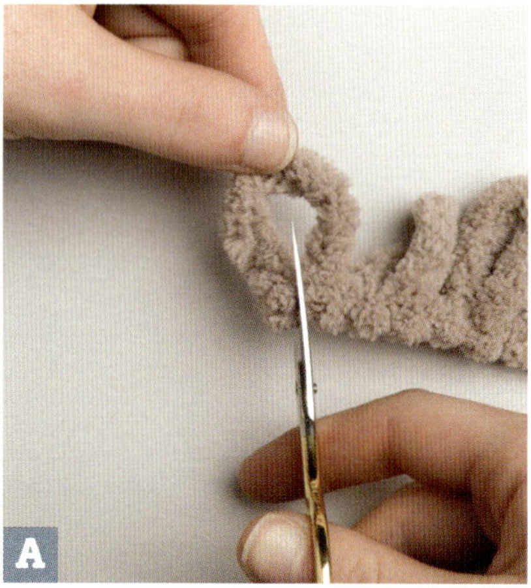

A

To begin, open the first loop by cutting the center to create a longer length for weaving in the end. **(PHOTOS A and B)**

Count 10 loops, this is the '*cast on*'. **(PHOTO C)**

Row 1: Work this row from **right** to **left**, with the working yarn in the back.

B

Hold loop 10 (from the cast on) in your left hand. With your right hand, pass loop 11, from the working yarn, from **back** to **front** through loop 10. **(PHOTOS D and E)**

The first '***knit***' stitch has been created.

Pull the loop all the way up. It will help the next row flow easier.

Move to loop 9 on the cast on, grab the next loop (from the working yarn) and pass the loop from **back** to **front** through loop 9 to complete the next knit stitch.

To work the next stitch, pass the next loop (from the working yarn) through the next loop on the cast on row from **back** to **front**.

Repeat to the end of the cast on.

You should have 10 stitches (loops) after working this row. **(PHOTO F)**

The first row is the trickiest! It will get easier.

F

G

Row 2: Work this row from **left** to **right**, with the working yarn in the **back** (do **not** turn the work). **(PHOTO G)**

Pass the next loop from the working yarn, from **back** to **front**, through the first stitch on the previous row. **(PHOTO H)**

Pass the next working loop from **back** to **front** through the next stitch on the previous row.

Repeat this to the end of the previous row.

You should have 10 stitches (loops) after working this row.

Always count your stitches after working each row. If you do not have 10 stitches, you have skipped working a stitch on the previous row.

Simply pull on the working yarn, removing each loop from the stitches, until you reach the skipped stitch; then finish working the row.

Row 3: Work this row from **right** to **left**, with the working yarn in the **back**.

Pass the next working loop from **back** to **front** through the first stitch on the previous row.

Pass the next working loop from **back** to **front** through the next stitch on the previous row.

Repeat this to the end of the row.

You should have 10 stitches after working this row.

Rows 4-60: Repeat Row 2 and 3, 28 times; then repeat Row 2 once **more** ***(see Joining a New Skein/ Changing Colors, page 19)***.

Feel free to alter the length by using more or less rows to make the scarf the size you want.

Once you have finished your last row it is time to '***bind off***'.

After working Row 60 you will have 10 loops and the working yarn with be on the right end.

Binding Off Stitches

Cut the working yarn 2 loops **past** the last stitch. **(PHOTO I)**

Cut open the 2 loops so that you will have a long tail.

Beginning with the first stitch (loop) at the edge **OPPOSITE** the long tail (on the left side) **(PHOTO J)**, pull up the second stitch through the first stitch from **back** to **front**.

I

J

You have bound off the first stitch. **(PHOTO K)**

Pull the next stitch through the current stitch from **back** to **front**, and repeat this step until each stitch has been bound off and only one stitch remains. **(PHOTOS L, M and N)**

Bring the long tail completely through the remaining stitch. **(PHOTO O)**

Thread your yarn or tapestry needle with the long ends and weave them back and forth through the back of the stitches.

N

O

*When your working yarn ends on the left edge, the process will be the same, but you will work from **right** to **left**.*

Before we move on, take a look at your piece. There is a front and a back side to the work.

Do you see the 'V' stitch, or ones that look like interlocked teardrops? That is the front (or **right** side) of your work. **(PHOTO P)**

On the back you'll see horizontal lines and that's the back (or **wrong** side) of the work. **(PHOTO Q)**

Joining a New Skein/Changing Colors

When your first skein comes to an end, or if you want to change to a different color, you will need to join a second skein.

Cut the last loop of the first skein (just as you did the first loop when beginning the scarf). **(PHOTO R)**

Next, cut the first loop of the new skein and knot the 2 ready loops as close as you can get them. This will make the work 'seamless' and you can continue with the pattern. **(PHOTOS S and T)**

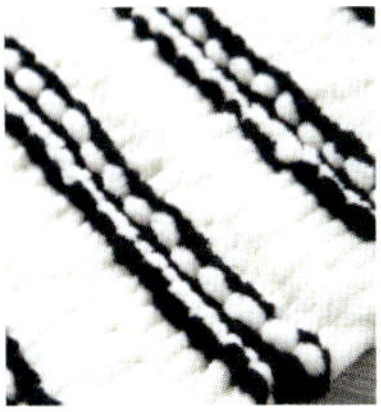
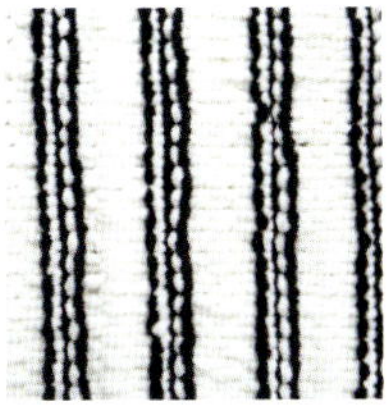

Rug

BASIC

Now that you've mastered the knit stitch while making your scarf, let's move onto the purl stitch. We will be using 2 colors, which will allow you to see the texture of the new stitch. The purl stitch will give you options of adding texture and detail to any project...just like this rug!

Approximate Finished Size:
42" wide x 24" high (106.5 cm x 61 cm)

SHOPPING LIST

Yarn (Jumbo Weight) JUMBO 7

[6.4 ounces, 18 yards
(180 grams, 16 meters) per skein]:

- ☐ Cream - 2 skeins
- ☐ Black - 1 skein

Additional Supplies

- ☐ Scissors
- ☐ Large eye tapestry or yarn needle

INSTRUCTIONS

To begin, open the first loop by cutting the center to create a longer length for weaving in the end.

With Cream, cast on 44 loops.

Row 1: Work this row from **right** to **left**, with the working yarn in the **back**.

Hold loop 44 in your left hand.

With your right hand, pass loop 45 from **back** to **front** through loop 44, creating your first '***knit***' stitch, knit each stitch across. **(PHOTO A)**

A

At the end of the row, cut the yarn 2 loops **past** the last working stitch; join Black ***(see Joining a New Skein/Changing Colors, page 19)***. **(PHOTO B)**

Row 2: Work this row from **left** to **right**, with the working yarn in the **front** (do **not** turn the work).

*When you **'purl'**, the yarn will always be in the **front** of your work.*

Pass the next loop from the working yarn, from **front** to **back,** through the first stitch on the previous row. **(PHOTO C)**

The first '***purl***' stitch has been created.

Pass the next loop, from **front** to **back**, through the next stitch on the previous row.

Repeat this to the end of the previous row. **(PHOTOS D and E)**

You should have 44 stitches (loops) after working this row.

At the end of the row, cut the yarn 2 loops **past** the last working stitch; join Cream.

Row 3: Work this row from **right** to **left**, with the working yarn in the **front**. **(PHOTO F)**

Purl each stitch across. **(PHOTO G)**

F

G

Row 4: Working from **left** to **right** with the yarn in the **back**, knit each stitch across.

Remember that when you ***knit****, the working yarn will need to be in the* ***back*** *of the work.*

Row 5: Working from **right** to **left** with the yarn in the **back**, knit each stitch across; cut the yarn 2 loops **past** the last working stitch; join Black.

Rows 6-28: Repeat Rows 2-5, 5 times; then repeat Rows 2-4 once **more**.

Row 29: Working from **right** to **left** with the yarn in the **back**, knit each stitch across.

Once you have finished Row 29 and you have 44 loops with the working yarn on the left, it is time to ***'bind off'***.

Cut the working yarn 2 loops **past** the last working stitch. Cut open the 2 loops so that you will have a long tail.

Beginning with the first stitch (loop) at the edge **OPPOSITE** the long tail (on the right side), pull up the second stitch through the first stitch from **back** to **front**. You have bound off the first stitch.

Pull the next stitch through the current stitch from **back** to **front**, and repeat this step until each stitch has been bound off and only one stitch remains.

Bring the long tail completely through the remaining stitch.

Thread your yarn or tapestry needle with the long ends and weave them back and forth through the back of the stitches.

Wrap

BASIC

We've now mastered the cast on, knit, purl, joining new skeins and bind off...let's keep learning! In this pattern you'll learn how to use the bind off in a unique way and how to yarn over and skip loops to create a pretty lacy wrap.

Approximate Finished Size:

15½" wide x 58" long (39.5 cm x 147.5 cm)

SHOPPING LIST

Yarn (Jumbo Weight)

[6.4 ounces, 18 yards
(180 grams, 16 meters) per skein]:

- ☐ 3 skeins

Additional Supplies

- ☐ Scissors
- ☐ Large eye tapestry or yarn needle

INSTRUCTIONS

To begin, open the first loop by cutting the center to create a longer length for weaving in the end.

Cast on 80 loops.

Row 1: Working from **right** to **left** with the yarn in the **back**, knit each stitch across.

Row 2: Working from **left** to **right** with the yarn in the **front** (do **not** turn the work), purl each stitch across. You should have 80 stitches (loops).

Row 3: Working from **right** to **left** with the yarn in the **back**, knit one stitch, ★ bind off the **next** stitch (**right** to **left**) *(see Binding Off Stitches, page 15)* **(PHOTO A)**,

skip the next **working** loop, then use the **next** working loop to knit the stitch (loop) that was created by the bind off **(PHOTO B)**.

Now, repeat from the ★ across the remainder of the row **(PHOTO C)**.

If you were to bind off a stitch and not skip one working loop, it would decrease the row by one stitch. We are creating a lacy and open look, not decreasing, so make sure you skip that working loop!

Row 4: Working from **left** to **right** with the yarn in the **back**, knit one stitch, ★ bind off the next stitch (**left** to **right**) **(PHOTO D)**, skip the next **working** loop, then use the **next** working loop to knit the stitch (loop) that was created by the bind off **(PHOTO E)**.

Now, repeat from the ★ across the remainder of the row.

Rows 5-13: Repeat Rows 3 and 4, 4 times; then repeat Row 3 once **more**.

D

Row 14: Working from **left** to **right** with the yarn in the **front**, purl each stitch across.

Row 15: Working from **right** to **left** with the yarn in the **back**, knit each stitch across.

Bind off **right** to **left** *(see Binding Off Stitches, page 15)*.

Bring the long tail completely through the remaining stitch.

Thread your yarn or tapestry needle with the long ends and weave them back and forth through the back of the stitches.

Cowl

BASIC

Don't run away when you see the word 'cable'....it's one of the easiest stitches you'll learn in this book! Seriously! It's as simple as taking the first stitch, crossing it in front or behind the second one and knitting them in order. It looks amazing, so jump in and make your own twisted cable cowl.

Approximate Finished Size:
28" wide x 9" high (71 cm x 23 cm)

SHOPPING LIST

Yarn (Jumbo Weight) JUMBO 7

[6.4 ounces, 18 yards
(180 grams, 16 meters) per skein**]**:

- ☐ Grey - 1 skein
- ☐ Cream - 1 skein

Additional Supplies

- ☐ Scissors
- ☐ 2" (5 cm) Buttons - 3
- ☐ Large eye tapestry or yarn needle
- ☐ Sewing needle and thread

INSTRUCTIONS

To begin, open the first loop by cutting the center to create a longer length for weaving in the end.

With Grey, cast on 42 loops.

Row 1: Working from **right** to **left** with the yarn in the **back**, knit the first stitch, ★ cross the **next** stitch in **front** of the following stitch (to the **left**) **(PHOTO A)**, knit the back stitch, then knit the front stitch **(Cable Left made)**;

repeat from the ★ across to the last stitch, knit the last stitch.

You will have worked one knit stitch at the beginning of the row, Cable Left 20 times, and one knit stitch at the end of the row.

A

Row 2: Working from **left** to **right** with the yarn in the **back** (do **not** turn the work), knit the first 2 stitches, ★ cross the next stitch in **front** of the following stitch (to the **right**) **(PHOTO B)**, knit the back stitch, then knit the front stitch **(Cable Right made)**;

repeat from the ★ across.

You will have worked 2 knit stitches at the beginning of the row and Cable Right 20 times.

Did you notice that the only difference between the two cables is the direction that the first stitch slants? **(PHOTOS D and E)**

Row 3: Working from **right** to **left** with the yarn in the **back**, knit the first stitch, work Cable Left across to the last stitch, knit the last stitch.

Row 4: Working from **left** to **right** with the yarn in the **back**, knit the first 2 stitches, work Cable Right across the remainder of the row.

Rows 5-9: Repeat Rows 3 and 4 twice, then repeat Row 3 once **more.**

D

E

Cut the Grey 2 loops **past** the last working stitch; join Cream *(see Joining A New Skein/Changing Colors, page 19)*.

Row 10: Working from **left** to **right** with the yarn in the **back**, knit the first 2 stitches, work Cable Right across the remainder of the row.

Row 11: Working from **right** to **left** with the yarn in the **back**, knit the first stitch, work Cable Left across to the last stitch, knit the last stitch.

Row 12: Working from **left** to **right** with the yarn in the **back**, knit the first 2 stitches, work Cable Right across the remainder of the row.

Bind off all stitches from **left** to **right** *(see Binding Off Stitches, page 15)*.

Bring the long tail completely through the remaining stitch.

Thread your yarn or tapestry needle with the long ends and weave them back and forth through the back of the stitches.

Using sewing needle and thread, sew the three buttons along one edge and button between the stitches on the opposite edge of the Cowl.

Basket

BASIC

While making this basket we are going to add even more stitches to our collection, and have fun along the way. When you finger knit, working in the round is easy and with this technique, you'll have a basket in no time.

Approximate Finished Size:
11" diameter x 8" high (28 cm x 20.5 cm)

SHOPPING LIST

Yarn (Jumbo Weight) JUMBO 7

[6.4 ounces, 18 yards
(180 grams, 16 meters) per skein]:

☐ 3 skeins

Additional Supplies

☐ Stitch marker
or scrap piece of yarn

☐ Scissors

☐ Large eye tapestry or yarn needle

INSTRUCTIONS

BASE

To begin, open the first two loops by cutting the center to create a longer length for tying and weaving in the end.

Cast on 4 loops. Tie a knot after the 4th loop to create a ring. **(PHOTO A)**

A

Round 1 (Increase round)**:** Working from **right** to **left** with the yarn in the **back**, pass the next 2 loops from the working yarn from **back** to **front** through each stitch around: 8 stitches. **(PHOTO B)**

*We are increasing the number of stitches on each round by working **'knit increases'.***

*Pulling more than one loop from **back** to **front** through a stitch will help us achieve the increase.*

Round 2: Working from **right** to **left** and beginning with the next unworked loop from the working yarn, bind off 8 stitches ***(see Binding Off Stitches, page 15)***; place a stitch marker or scrap piece of yarn in the remaining stitch. **(PHOTO C)**

B

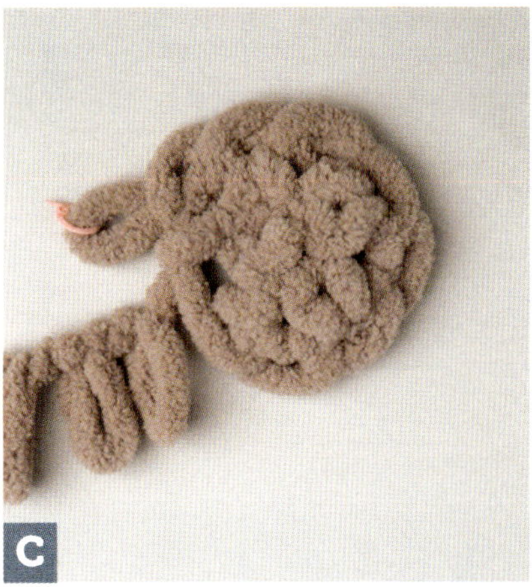
C

To 'pick up a stitch', pass the next loop from the working yarn from **back** to **front** under **both** loops of the next bound off stitch.

Round 3 (Increase round)**:** Working from **right** to **left** and leaving the marked stitch unworked, pick up 2 stitches from **back** to **front** under **both** loops of each bound off stitch around: 16 stitches and one marked stitch. **(PHOTO D)**

Round 4: Working from **right** to **left** and beginning with **the marked stitch (PHOTO D)**, bind off each stitch around; place previous stitch marker in the remaining stitch.

This technique allows the fabric of the basket to be thicker.

Round 5 (Increase round)**:** Working from **right** to **left**, leaving the marked stitch unworked and working under **both** loops of **each** bound off stitch **(now and throughout)**, ★ pick up one stitch in the next stitch, pick up 2 stitches in the next stitch; repeat from the ★ around: 24 stitches and one marked stitch.

Round 6: Working from **right** to **left** and leaving the marked stitch unworked, knit each stitch around.

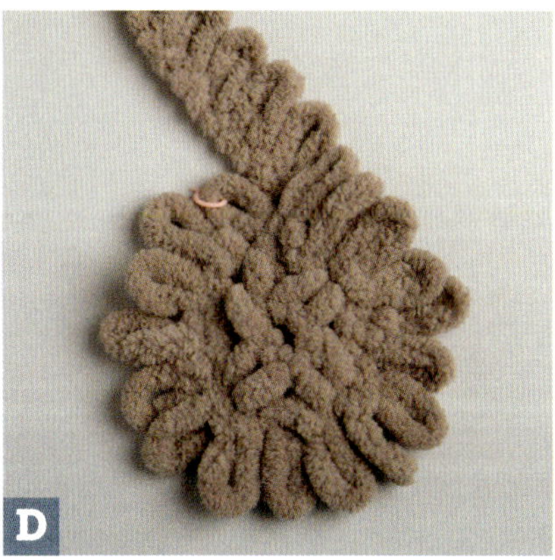

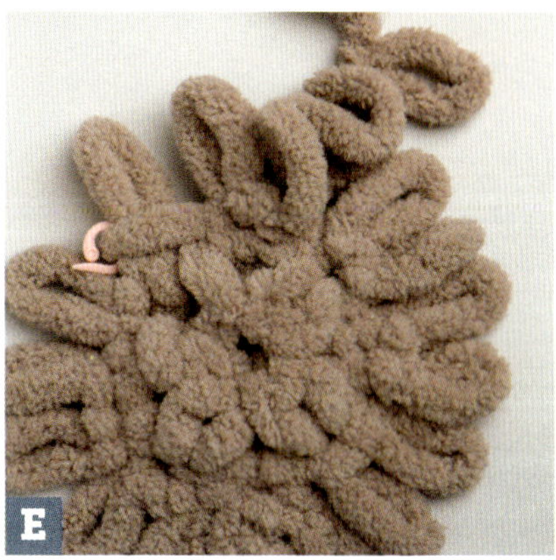

Round 7: Working from **right** to **left** and beginning with the marked stitch, bind off each stitch around; place previous stitch marker in the remaining stitch.

Round 8 (Increase round)**:** Working from **right** to **left** and leaving the marked stitch unworked, ★ pick up one stitch in **each of** the next 2 stitches, pick up 2 stitches in the next stitch; repeat from ★ around: 32 stitches and one marked stitch.

We are gradually increasing so that we have a large circular base.

Rounds 9 and 10: Repeat Rounds 6 and 7.

Round 11 (Increase round)**:** Working from **right** to **left** and leaving the marked stitch unworked, ★ pick up one stitch in **each of** the next 3 stitches, pick up 2 stitches in the next stitch; repeat from ★ around: 40 stitches and one marked stitch.

Rounds 12 and 13: Repeat Rounds 6 and 7.

Round 14 (Increase round)**:** Working from **right** to **left** and leaving the marked stitch unworked, ★ pick up one stitch in **each of** the next 4 stitches, pick up 2 stitches in the next stitch; repeat from ★ around: 48 stitches and one marked stitch.

Rounds 15 and 16: Repeat Rounds 6 and 7. **(PHOTO F)**

Cut the working yarn 2 loops **past** the last stitch. Cut open the 2 loops so that you will have a long tail.

Bring the long tail from **back** to **front** through the first bound off stitch of the round **and** through the remaining stitch.

F

BODY

Each bound off stitch has a ***'front loop'*** and a ***'back loop'***. **(PHOTO G)**

The **front loop** is the strand that is closest to you and the **back loop** is the strand that is **behind** the front loop (farther away from you).

When using just the back loop, the front loop will remain unworked and create a ***'turning ridge'*** so that the Basket will automatically turn upward instead of having a rounded base.

Open the first loop of the working yarn by cutting the center to create a longer length for weaving in the end.

Round 1: Working from **right** to **left**, pick up one loop in the back loop only of each stitch around: 48 stitches.

Round 2: Working from **right** to **left** and beginning with the next loop from the working yarn, knit each stitch around: 48 stitches.

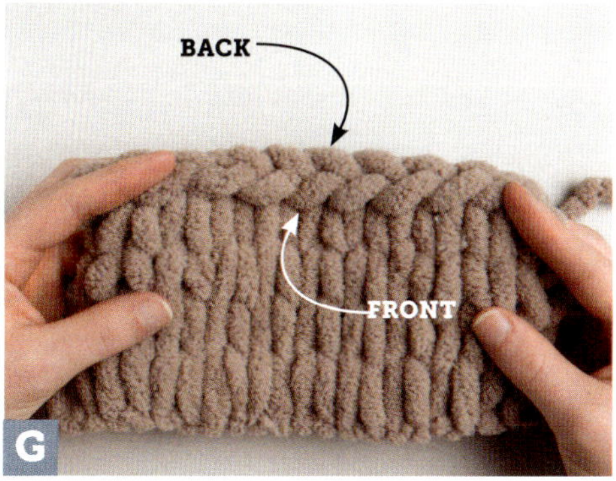

The Body is worked in the same manner as the Base.

Round 3: Working from **right** to **left** and beginning with the next unworked loop from the working yarn, bind off each stitch around; place a stitch marker in the remaining stitch.

Round 4: Working from **right** to **left** and leaving the marked stitch unworked, pick up one stitch in each stitch around: 48 stitches and one marked stitch.

Round 5: Working from **right** to **left** and leaving the marked stitch unworked, knit each stitch around.

Round 6: Working from **right** to **left** and beginning with the marked stitch, bind off each stitch around; place previous stitch marker in the remaining stitch.

Rounds 7-19: Repeat Rounds 4-6, 4 times; then repeat Round 4 once **more**.

To knit 2 stitches together, you are using 2 stitches to make them into one stitch. Place the next stitch in **front** of the following stitch, then pass the next loop from the working yarn through the 2 stitches from **back** to **front**, knitting them together as one stitch.

Round 20: Working from **right** to **left** and leaving the marked stitch unworked, ★ knit the next 4 stitches, knit 2 stitches together; repeat from ★ around: 40 stitches and one marked stitch.

Round 21: Working from **right** to **left** and beginning with the marked stitch, bind off each stitch around; place previous stitch marker in the remaining stitch.

Round 22: Working from **right** to **left** and leaving the marked stitch unworked, ★ skip the next 5 stitches, beginning with the 7th loop from the working yarn (you will skip the first 6 loops of the working yarn to form the handle), pick up one stitch in each of the next 15 stitches; repeat from the ★ once **more**: 30 stitches, 12 loops, and one marked stitch.

Round 23: Working from **right** to **left** and leaving the marked stitch unworked, ★ knit the next 6 loops, knit the next 15 stitches; repeat from the ★ once **more**: 42 stitches and one marked stitch.

Round 24: Working from **right** to **left** and beginning with the marked stitch, bind off each stitch around; cut the working yarn 2 loops **past** the remaining stitch.

Cut open the 2 loops so that you will have a long tail.

Bring the long tail from **back** to **front** through the first bound off stitch of the round **and** through the remaining stitch.

Thread your yarn or tapestry needle with the long ends and weave them back and forth through the back of the stitches.

Pet Bed

BASIC

This pet bed is a great way to practice many of your new stitches and techniques. We will start by making 2 panels, joining them together into a fluffy pillow (but don't stop there!), then we'll add a simple edge to finish. Now, you and your pet friends can enjoy your finger knitting!

Approximate Finished Size:
20" wide x 18" deep x 6" high (51 cm x 45.5 cm x 15 cm)

SHOPPING LIST

Yarn (Jumbo Weight) JUMBO 7

[6.4 ounces, 18 yards
(180 grams, 16 meters) per skein**]**:

- ☐ 3 skeins

Additional Supplies

- ☐ Stitch markers - 4 **or** scrap pieces of yarn
- ☐ Scissors
- ☐ Large eye tapestry or yarn needle
- ☐ 6-8 ounces (170-227 grams) polyester fiberfill

INSTRUCTIONS

PANEL (Make 2)

To begin, open the first loop by cutting the center to create a longer length for weaving in the end.

Cast on 25 loops.

Place a stitch marker or scrap piece of yarn around the **base** of the 8th and 18th loop of the cast on row to mark the rolled edge placement.

Row 1: Working from **right** to **left** with the yarn in the **back**, knit each stitch across.

Row 2: Working from **left** to **right** with the yarn in the **back**, knit each stitch across.

Rows 3-19: Repeat Rows 1 and 2, 8 times; then repeat Row 1 once **more**.

Bind off all stitches from **right** to **left** *(see* ***Binding Off Stitches, page 15****)*.

Bring the long tail completely through the remaining stitch.

These Panels are very basic and a great way to practice your knit stitch. **(PHOTO A)**

When you're finished, lay them with the ***back*** *sides together. Match up the stitch markers and find the first and last stitch of the row (do* ***not*** *remove the markers). This will be where you pull the loops through to join the Panels.* **(PHOTO B)**

ASSEMBLY

Open the first loop to create a long end.

Beginning in any corner, working from **left** to **right** and through **both** layers of **both** Panels, pull up 22 loops along **each** side, stuffing the piece with polyester fiberfill before pulling up all of the loops on the last edge: 88 loops. **(PHOTO C)**

Do you see how the stitches come through both panels? **(PHOTO D)**

Working from **left** to **right**, bind off all of the stitches around. **(PHOTO E)**

Cut the working yarn 2 loops **past** the remaining stitch. Cut open the 2 loops so that you will have a long tail.

Bring the long tail from **back** to **front** through the first bound off stitch of the round **and** through the remaining stitch.

Tip: You may want to bind off stitches as you pull up the loops to make sure the loops don't come out.

C

D

E

ROLLED EDGE

Row 1: With the yarn in the **front** and the same side of the piece facing, working from **right** to **left** and through **both** loops of the bound off stitches, pick up a stitch from **front** to **back** in the marked 8th stitch on the cast on row; pick up the next 7 stitches from **front** to **back** (ending at first corner), **(PHOTO F)**

★ pick up 22 stitches evenly spaced from **front** to **back** (ending at next corner); repeat from the ★ 2 times **more**, pick up the next 8 stitches from **front** to **back**, ending in the marked 18th stitch on cast on row: 82 stitches. **(PHOTO G)**

Turn the piece **over** so that the other side is facing you.

Row 2: Working from **right** to **left**, knit each stitch across.

Row 3: Beginning with the first stitch of Row 2, bind off all stitches from **right** to **left**: one stitch remains.

Row 4: Counting the remaining stitch as the first stitch, and working from **back** to **front** under **both** loops of **each** bound off stitch **(now and throughout)**, pull up a loop from **left** to **right** in each stitch across: 82 stitches.

F

Row 5: Working from **right** to **left**, with yarn in **front**, purl each stitch across.

Row 6: Beginning with the first stitch of Row 5, bind off all stitches from **right** to **left**: one stitch remains.

Row 7: Counting the remaining stitch as the first stitch, pull up a loop from **left** to **right** in each stitch across: 82 stitches.

To knit 2 stitches together, you are using 2 stitches to make them into one stitch. Place the next stitch in **front** of the following stitch, then pass the next loop from the working yarn through the 2 stitches from **back** to **front**, knitting them together as one stitch.

Row 8: Working from **right** to **left**, knit the first 10 stitches, knit 2 stitches together, ★ knit the next 4 stitches, knit 2 stitches together; repeat from the ★ across to the last 10 stitches, knit the last 10 stitches: 71 stitches.

Row 9: Beginning with the first stitch of Row 8, bind off all stitches from **right** to **left**: one stitch remains.

Row 10: Counting the remaining stitch as the first stitch, pull up a loop from **left** to **right** in each stitch across: 71 stitches.

Row 11: Working from **right** to **left**, with yarn in **front**, purl each stitch across.

Row 12: Beginning with the first stitch of Row 11, bind off all stitches from **right** to **left**: one stitch remains.

Row 13: Counting the remaining stitch as the first stitch, pull up a loop from **left** to **right** in each stitch across: 71 stitches.

Row 14: Working from **right** to **left**, knit each stitch across.

Row 15: Beginning with the first stitch of Row 14, bind off all stitches from **right** to **left**: one stitch remains. **(PHOTO H)**

Cut open 30 loops so that you will have a long tail for sewing. Bring the long tail completely through the remaining stitch.

Thread your yarn or tapestry needle with the long end and insert the needle through the last bound off stitch **and** the bottom of the seam you created when you joined the two panels. **(PHOTOS I and J)**

Then, push the needle back up through the seam and come through the next bound off stitch. **(PHOTO K)**

Repeat in this manner across the Rolled Edge, making sure the 8 stitches on each side of the front are aligned.

Sew the end of the rows together on each side; then tack the middle of the rolled cuff to the pillow for stability; secure the end.

I

J

K

We have made every effort to ensure that these instructions are accurate and complete. We cannot, however, be responsible for human error, typographical mistakes, or variations in individual work.

Production Team: Instructional/Technical Editor - Linda A. Daley; Senior Graphic Artist - Lora Puls; Photo Stylist - Lori Wenger; and Photographer - Jason Masters.

Made in U.S.A.